Building a Great Children's Ministry

Building a Great Children's Ministry

Evelyn M. R. Johnson
Bobbie Bower

Creative Leadership Series

Lyle E. Schaller, Editor

Abingdon Press / Nashville

BUILDING A GREAT CHILDREN'S MINISTRY

Copyright © 1992 by Abingdon Press

All rights reserved.

This book is printed on acid-free recycled paper.

Library of Congress Cataloging-in-Publication Data

Evelyn M. R. Johnson
    Building a great children's ministry / Evelyn M. R. Johnson, Bobbie Bower.
    p.   cm. — (Creative leadership series)
    ISBN 0-687-03388-8
    1. Christian education of children. 2. Church work with children. I. Johnson, Evelyn M. R. II. Title. III. Series.
BV1475.2.b68   1992
268'.432—dc20   92-7817
                                                    CIP

Sections of this book are adapted from previous publications prepared by the authors for The Evangelical General Church, Chicago, Illinois: *Assessing the Teaching-Learning Process: For Churches* by Bobbie Bower; *Choosing Curriculum Materials for Children's Programming in Covenant Churches* by Bobbie Bower and Evelyn M. R. Johnson; *Helping Churches to Be Safer Places for Children; Infant Toddler Ministry* by Bobbie Bower.

MANUFACTURED IN THE UNITED STATES OF AMERICA

To Eric, Craig, Jonathan, Betsy, and Jeremy,
who made the concept of children
real in our lives

Foreword

Do we need another book on children's ministry? Many congregations have more books on children's ministries in the church library than they have children in the Sunday school. No, we do not need another book on children's ministry.

What is needed is a book on children's ministry in today's world, not another book on how to do ministry in 1962.

What's the difference? The difference is that today we have a new and different generation of parents who have given birth to a new generation of children. Back in 1987 the United States entered into what is the second biggest baby boom in American history—and the numbers may exceed the 1956–1962 peak of the earlier baby boom. This new baby boom is producing huge numbers of children for the churches' nurseries, Sunday schools, music programs, early childhood development centers, and Parents' Day Out. In 1980 the American population included 3.2 million five-year-olds. In 1996 that number will be 4.2 million.

The parents of today's two-year-olds and seven-year-olds are not carbon copies of the young parents of the children of the late 1950s and the 1960s. Those youngsters are the parents of this new generation of children. This new generation of parents married later in life than did their parents, they were older when that first baby was born, they are better educated, they are more likely to be two-income families, and they have higher expectations of the quality of their church's ministry.

They choose a church home, not on the basis of inherited loyalties or denominational affiliation or geographical convenience, but rather on how responsive a church is to their religious needs and the needs of their children. That search for a church home often begins with the church nursery; too often that first visit motivates the parents to keep looking. Likewise they seek an attractive learning environment for their children. A frequent expression of that search is the hope, "I want my kids to get more out of Sunday school than I did when I was their age."

In broader terms, many of these parents are fully aware of the transformation of American society from the child-centered world of 1957 to the adult-oriented culture of the 1990s. They recognize that today's society is an increasingly barren, and often hostile, environment for the rearing of children. They seek a church that places a high value on children and acts out that value system.

This book tells how to create a healthy environment for children in your church. That requires healthy relationships.

The co-authors combine two threads. One is an engrossing story that will capture and hold the reader's attention. The other thread is the wealth of specific suggestions on how to build and maintain that healthy environment for children's ministry that is a top priority for a growing proportion of this generation of new parents.

LYLE E. SCHALLER
Yokefellow Institute

Contents

TO BE A CHILD

To be a child
  is to be . . .
    young,
    playful,
    innocent,
    dependent,
    hopeful,
    connected.

To be a child
  is to believe . . .
    that someone bigger than you will
      help you,
      protect you,
      teach you,
      share in your joy,
      care if you hurt,
      be there for you,
      love you completely.

To be a child
  is to become.

Preface

Since 1976 our lives have intersected in various settings to provide direction and support for those involved in children's ministry. We have led regional workshops and served together in a local church setting. We have shared a variety of writing projects and provided guidance for expanding children's ministry in our own denomination. Through these experiences we developed strong convictions about the value of a child and increased our commitment to developing parent-church partnerships.

This book became a challenge for us to sort out and express in words our approach to ministry with children. It provided an opportunity to bring together our varied knowledge and experiences in early and middle childhood, the spiritual formation of children, adult education, local church planning, and ministry with volunteers.

Throughout this book, readers will find examples and case stories with names. Alterations were made to protect confidentiality. Yet, we have attempted to preserve the accuracy of the human dynamics or principles involved.

Every attempt was made to apply insights of noted researchers regarding the baby-boomer generation and characteristics of today's children. The ideas shared in these areas represent our understanding of thoughts shared by many others. The planning process outlined, the programming options suggested, and the various checklists are adaptations of our work during a recent denominational emphasis on children's ministry.

We want to thank Lyle and Agnes Schaller, who invited us to write this book. His gentle prodding "to write instead of sleep" and her anticipation of the finished product have kept us on task.

We are deeply thankful for the children's ministry staffs within the Evangelical Covenant Church. They have welcomed us as workshop leaders, "tested out" our approaches, and provided needed encouragement many times.

Finally, we express sincere appreciation to the people who really made this book happen! They are our spouses and children. They have unselfishly granted us the privilege of time together since our paths first crossed in 1976. In those times we have generated ideas and lived out dreams.

Evelyn M. R. Johnson
Bobbie Bower

I

Who Are the Children?

The Reverend Watkins sat before the empty pews. It was customary on this morning for the minister to be in the sanctuary early. Praying for the people of the congregation and community was a priority. The minister visualized the people who had been there only a few days before.

The children from the children's choir sat on the front two rows. Their eager faces and squirming bodies brought a smile to the minister's face. Children were an important part of this worshiping congregation. Many of these children were part of seemingly healthy families within the congregation. Yet, even among the healthiest, the minister realized there were potential difficulties.

Sarah's parents had been in for counscling last week. Jeff's mother seemed to "live" at the church, and the pastor knew this was causing conflict at home. Todd was a very special child within this congregation. His birth occurred after fifteen years of marriage. The church family had helped support the couple during the difficult years of infertility.

In the second row were five children who looked totally unrelated but were all living in the same family. They were part of a foster family within the congregation. Three were officially adopted, and the other two were in process. These children also were very special to the church. In turn, the church was a special place of healing for them. At the end of the row, two cousins sat together. Their mothers had grown up in the area and had remained here, a rarity in this mobile society. The pastor also knew that one family had a job offer in a community twelve hundred miles away. This was a time of important decisions for them.

Next to the cousins was the children's choir director, a single parent raising two children. The image of the choir director reminded the pastor of the request for a parenting class for single parents.

After the children sang, many older children scattered among the worshiping community to find family members. The younger ones met in the rear of the sanctuary and went to Children's Church. The minister remembered the Bradleys' look of relief as their young grandchildren exited. The Bradleys were caring for these children while their daughter was in a substance-abuse rehabilitation center. The father had not contacted the children in more than a year.

The Bradleys usually sat with their longtime

16

friends, the O'Neills. The O'Neills helped the Bradleys care for their grandchildren. This week they were visiting their own grandchildren seven hundred miles away. Rumors have suggested that the O'Neills may be moving closer to their children when they retire next year. Such a move would be especially sad for the Bradleys.

Sitting behind the Bradleys were the Jemisons, who seem to come only when the children's choir sings. The pastor realized that the Jemison children were close in age to the Bradley grandchildren. This might be a good point of contact and friendship. It might be a way of helping the Jemisons become more involved within the church family.

The minister's gaze traveled to the other side of the room. The Reynoldses were in church. This was a second marriage for both adults. They had just had a new baby. The father's daughter, Michelle, was visiting from out of state. The terrible custody battle over Michelle continued, with much emotional pain and financial expense. The present arrangements allow visits on alternating holiday vacations and one weekend a month during the school year.

Along the side aisle was Stacy Andrews. She came each week with her baby. She had not felt welcomed in her other church as a single, teen mother. An older family friend, Miss Thompson, suggested she try this church. Last week she brought a friend.

The Garcias sat near the back of the church. A new family was visiting with them. Mr. Garcia is the director of a mission outreach center located in the core of the urban center. He and his wife lead a Bible study during the week. Occasionally members of the group attend church here.

The minister continued to remember their faces and prayed for the people and names that came to mind. Slowly walking up the aisle, the minister noticed creatively folded church bulletins on several pews. From down the hall came sounds of excitement and sadness as parents, teachers, and children said their hellos and good-byes. The child-care center sponsored by the church was open for another day.

The minister unlocked the door to the offices. The day's calendar was open on the desk. Tonight the trustees would meet to discuss facility modifications to accommodate new areas of ministry. The newspaper was open to the church's advertisement for a home safety class designed for first-time parents. The minister checked the wording to see if it was consistent with the sign posted on the church property.

The Reverend Watkins looked out the window. In the distance was a school bus. Cars moved back and forth. With eyes closed, the minister again prayed. "Oh, God. Help us to really minister in the lives of children."

★ ★ ★ ★

There are universal characteristics that identify a person as a child. They transcend generations but are interpreted in culture. To be a child is special. Children are not immediately aware of their special nature. This awareness develops as they respond to those who touch their lives in significant ways. It creates attitudes about self and relationships in all of life. Jesus drew adult attention to the intrinsic value and worth of children. He chose the child to create new ways for thinking about God's kingdom. He showed that children's opportunity "to be" depends upon the people who surround them.

Children are both powerful and powerless. It is within this tension that their vulnerability is created. Six major characteristics highlight this vulnerability today. They include size, age, innocence, dependency, potential, and relationships.

Size

Children demand personal attention. The smaller the children, the more willing people are to be physically imposed upon by them. Infant cries bring people running. Adults hold, cuddle, and rock children at all hours of the day and night. They carry them in their arms, on their backs, and on their shoulders. They crawl around with them on "all fours."

Children draw adults into new relationships. People with children seem to gravitate to one another in parks, shopping malls, restaurants, and churches. Strangers initiate immediate conversations over the common topic of children and their development.

People absorb the financial impact of children. "Little people" need special equipment, materials, food, and clothing. People redesign space in homes and churches to meet children's needs. Parents hire caregivers to care for their children throughout the week. Bills for health care are a regular occurrence. Expenses continue as children discover toy supermarkets, fancy footwear, and fast food.

While children can command much attention, it may only be superficial. When compared to the time and resources invested in youth and adults, children may seem insignificant or lower in priority.

A child's power to initiate contact through smiles, tugs, hugs, conversation, and questions is expanded or diminished by the recipients of their attention. Children often find themselves powerless in a world where people merely tolerate or ignore them. The significant adults in their lives pursue their own desires. Children are "along for the ride" in the parents' fast lane. Serious neglect of children exists in many homes and churches.

Age

Before the late nineteenth century, people viewed children as miniature adults. Adults expected children, by the time they were eight to ten years of age, to labor equally with them in the factories and fields. Few persons gave regard to a child's limited thought processes or other areas of development. In the middle of the twentieth century, researchers in child development provided the world with much information related to child growth and maturity. This information reshaped educational and social systems. Persons began to value childhood as a unique, special time of life. "Ages" and "stages" were important. Educators and parents had information on reasonable expectations of children. This knowledge helped decide curriculum and educational placement in schools and churches. Being at a certain age level meant certain parental expectations for behavior. "Act your age" became a much used phrase.

Certain milestones and celebrations connect with age. Family and friends create much fanfare on the first birthday or at the formal entrance into school at age five or six. In some faith communities a specific age allows children to be baptized or confirmed, join the church, and partake of the communion elements.

A great privilege of childhood is spontaneous play. It is a powerful vehicle to help children understand their world. It helps children reduce stress, sort out life's relationships, and practice emerging skills and abilities. Adults often see play as opportunities to escape the responsibilities and realities of life. For children, play is their life. The power to play, without guilt, is the one part of childhood that adults often regret losing.

Manufacturers and retailers recognize the power of the "under 12" age group. This is not a new distinction. For many years, restaurants offered children's menus, entertainment activities provided reduced rates, and cereal boxes contained special gadgets and promotions.

Now there are fewer clear distinctions between adult and child consumption and responsibilities.

Retailers target children as a highly lucrative market. The fall 1990 issue of *Media and Values* noted that "some thirty-seven million children ages four to twelve control nearly nine billion dollars of their own money." Children shop for themselves and for the family. Advertisers and products discourage a "wait until you are older" philosophy. Adult clothing, activities, products, and equipment are sized down for children. A major sports magazine has developed a children's edition.

Delayed gratification is practically nonexistent. Activities, both positive and negative, previously associated with the teen years are now occurring in the elementary school. A local paper recently reported a church party held for preteens, ages 6 to 12. At-risk behaviors common among older elementary children include drug and alcohol experimentation and abuse. Intimate sexual relationships, eating disorders, and gang-related activity continue to increase among persons in this age group.

Children are hurried through life. The intensity of many children's social calendars equals that of success-oriented adults. Participation in sports, music, camps, and formal education is increasing for younger ages. Children are so over-programmed in our society that spontaneous play with a friend is rare. The church often contributes to this stressful state through its expectations of children and program schedules. Too often, children walk around as miniature adults. To "act one's age" is meaningless. What is there to look forward to in growing up?

Innocence

Children enter the world ready for discovery. Their lack of knowledge and perspective provides the basis for some humorous anecdotes. For example, in preparation for a children's sermon introducing Lent, the teacher tested the content with the children in the family. "What is Lent?" the teacher asked. The child's serious reply was, "Isn't it that stuff you get out of the dryer?"

Children's innocence creates a power to believe. They intuitively believe in others, especially bigger people. During early years, they assume these people must be right. Older children become more suspect of others. They have more knowledge and experience. Their reason for trust in someone can disappear.

Children expect the adults surrounding them to give necessary protection and guidance. Traditionally, helping a child to be a child meant limiting their contact with knowledge and experiences. Adults believed children lacked the ability to process information and experiences in the same manner as themselves. Now, more than ever before, children need both protection and guidance.

Television and mass communication have changed life for children and families. Before television, children were quite reliant upon older persons to provide information about the world beyond their homes, neighborhoods, and schools. Although the ability to read opened a whole new world of information, the content closely matched their level of understanding. The child dismissed things not understood or left them to imagining.

Television viewing exposes children to many unfiltered experiences. Children receive information for which they are ill prepared. Adults often under-supervise. No one processes the information with children. No one interprets it within the context of Christian values. There is no need for imagination. The electronic visualizations become all too real. They undermine the child's basic feeling of security. Adults do not seem able or willing to help.

In times past, adults protected most children from stressful family information. "Go play for a while" meant the discussion was not for children. Children should be informed of significant family changes such as divorce, terminal illness, and loss of job. These are some of the deep sadnesses that occur in life. Unfortunately, however, adults sometimes give children intimate details that are unnecessary. This provides a source of relief and venting for the parent, but its impact can be stressful for children. Important roles reverse when children provide emotional support for parents.

The most tragic loss of innocence in society today is in the prevalence of child abuse and, in particular, sexual abuse. This is the highest violation of the protection and guidance that children should expect of the adults in their lives. Abusive situations cross all economic, racial, geographic, and religious indices. It happens both in and outside our churches.

Dependency

Dependency is powerful because it engages other people's time and feelings. Children need support from significant adults in their lives. Adult members of the family have major physical and financial responsibility. They provide basic needs such as shelter, food, clothing, and supervision. Children respond to the nurturing ways in which physical needs are met. If needs are met in loving ways, children develop healthy attitudes of faith, hope, and love that sustain them through life.

People need to know that someone is there who really cares. This is how trust develops and grows. In the consistent giving and receiving of loving attention by child and adult, powerful bonds of human love develop. This provides the basis for developing a trusting relationship to God. Children's dependency gives them great power to trust.

Children's reliance upon significant adults in their lives is rapidly shifting to peers and material substitutes at earlier ages. Children are recipients of toys, gadgets, and expensive clothing as substitutes for lack of personal contact with adults. Elementary schools are establishing mental health teams. These teams include teachers, social workers, counselors, psychologists, administrators, and health professionals. They help children cope with emotional and social voids.

Due to employment, many adult family members are not physically available to their children throughout the day. There is greater dependence on sources outside the family for the direct provision of care. Children are part of various child-care arrangements, including parental flex-time.

Even parents who are home during the day use child care services. The "stay at home parent" participates in church, community, and personal enrichment activities. Large portions of their child's time may be spent in the care of someone else. Child care cooperatives; preschools; parents day out; and drop-off care at churches, shopping malls, and athletic centers help to accommodate this daytime life-style.

Some mothers choose to be home with their children during the younger years, but seek employment when their children are old enough to be in school all day. These families may use school-age child care programs where they exist. However, an increasing number of elementary-age children go home to an empty house. They spend their "unwind time" in isolation or with the responsibilities of caring for younger siblings and household management chores.

Self-reliance is an important part of the maturing process in children. But self-reliance should not be equated with self-care. Helping children to assume responsibility within the household is healthy to a point. They need adequate support and nurture during the process. Allowing children to be "on their own" may include preparing their own meals, finding their own transportation, and having sole responsibility for the care of younger siblings. This is beyond what should be expected of children.

Children intuitively associate the level of their parents' personal concern and involvement in their lives with their definition of love. Children want to depend upon the parent to be there to share in their joy and care if they hurt. Personal, uncluttered time is probably the most valued investment given to establish and support a relationship. Quality versus quantity time is a misnomer. It is not an either/or situation. It is both quality and quantity that make a difference in children's lives. Adults need to realize what children already know.

Potential

Adults expect children to "become." They are in process of being molded and shaped by inner and outer forces within their environment and their genetic code. No one knows the outcome. Therefore, the possibilities create tremendous power.

Some view children as the persons who will change the world in order to create a brighter and better tomorrow. Some see children as the hope for fixing the wrongs of past generations. Others believe children will heal broken relationships. Others envision children as necessary for the future care of an aging population. Some see children as extensions of themselves, the ones who will fulfill their unfulfilled dreams and hopes. In the Christian community, persons often view children as the future hope of the church.

The opportunity to point children in the "right" direction from the very beginning is highly motivating for some. Therefore, people are willing to invest time and financial resources in children. They will give physical and emotional energy to assure a better future. Children represent a powerful hope!

Adults are the influencers and shapers of children's lives. They both under-invest and over-invest in children's lives. Those who under-invest engage in neglectful behavior. The results are inadequate nutrition, inappropriate clothing, and delayed health and dental care. These deficiencies occur even within affluent households. In this case, the adults often give too much decision-making responsibility to children or place too little focus on the child.

In the indulgent household, the words "No" or "Wait" are seldom heard. Children are not held accountable for their actions. Children never learn there are boundaries in life, because the home has few, if any. The results of overindulgence are disastrous for the child, the family, and society.

Many adults believe "you can have it all." They are raising children with the same attitudes. This robs children of recognizing that one needs to set priorities and make choices. For the child, learning to choose is a critical life skill. In daily life events children need to gradually discover what it means to choose living and growing as a child of God.

Relationships

The birth of a child creates parents. Relationships are formed with generations of others who have brought them to this point. Persons who have not related well often come together around a child. Children are the incredible link between who has come before and who will be next. Their presence has a way of transcending time and space.

Children create stability for the family and its heritage. Note the wonder a great-grandparent has in holding the newest little relative, a child loved before being seen. Consider the grandparent who changes personal plans to provide long-term care for a grandchild. The greatest power within any relationship is love. Children have immense power to both give and receive it.

Children bring out the best and worst in adults. Their situations can produce intense frustration or delight; profound sorrow or joy. With children in their midst, adults find fresh meaning in the phrase "child of God" and in what it means to live out that loving, tender relationship.

The concept of "family" is in process. Children today grow up in a myriad of family structures. Some live with mother, father, brothers and/or sisters. More likely there is only one other sibling or the person is an only child. Other children live with one parent, probably their mother. Many live in blended families, which create their own set of complications and stress. Others live with grandparents who have adopted them because their own parents could no longer care for them. Others live with grandparents and their teen parent or foster-care families.

Many aspects of the family structure may change. Yet there can be constancy. The commonality within these varied structures is the opportunity for

29

children to feel and know love. Love cannot be institutionalized. It cannot be bartered. Healthy relationships give evidence of love. When family relationships center around an understanding of God's love and forgiveness, the child and the parent will be empowered to become all that God originally intended.

Children are not a right. "Children are a gift of the Lord" (Psalm 127:3). Creation is a miracle. The responsibility to care and nurture this unique miracle, the child, can have powerful effects. It can move a person from a self-absorbing "me" orientation to an inclusive "we" perspective. The responsibility helps one to recognize that being human means living within loving relationships. The church must be a powerful presence to help this maturing process.

II

Who Are the Adults in Children's Lives?

The doctor confirmed it! After seven years of marriage, Bill and Jane, both age thirty-two, will become parents of their first child. Planning for the future dominates their thinking. Since their own births in the sixties, the preparation for a child has changed. Bill and Jane's "to do" list includes:

_____Schedule parental leaves
_____Discuss flex-time possibilities at work
_____Check on reservation at child-care center
_____Call Bill's parents in Boston
_____Call Jane's mother and stepfather in Seattle
_____Write to Jane's father
_____Find a new home with an outdoor play area
_____Register for the hospital's childbirth class
_____Check on home-safety class at local church

Many changes in our society have added items to their list that were unknown by their parents. However, the changes during preparation may seem minimal when they experience the upcoming changes during the child's life, birth through age twelve.

Remembering When . . .

Bill grew up in a rural Midwestern community. Holidays were gala affairs with grandparents, aunts, uncles, and cousins gathered for meals and hours of playing games. When his mother worked part time, one of his grandmothers served as the caregiver. Although his family changed residences frequently, they always stayed within an hour's driving distance, allowing frequent visits with relatives and close friends. Evening hours with his parents included playing games together and watching favorite television programs such as "Father Knows Best." Weekends included frequent interaction with neighborhood children and their parents. When his family moved, they quickly became involved in church activities. Often, their denomination did not have a church in the new location. Bill's annual participation at a regional summer camp helped maintain a strong tie to the denomination.

Jane's early childhood years spent in a small town in the Pacific Northwest were similar to Bill's. She walked to and from school, often stopping by her father's business on the way home. Her secure world changed during the third grade, when her parents divorced. Her father moved his business to a major metropolitan area. Jane was able to visit him only once a month. Uncles, neighbors, and teachers filled the "father role" in her life. The members of her mother's church provided limited support. Few persons had experience in relating to a child from a divorced family. When Jane was in the sixth grade, her mother's remarriage provided a new sense of security, at least economically. Jane began to set career goals early. She hoped to avoid being dependent on relatives and friends as her mother had been.

Bill and Jane experienced many changes during their childhood. Yet the presence of supportive, caring adults was constant. Involvement with these adults helped shape a strong sense of identity for integrating into a rapidly changing adult world of the eighties. They wonder now who will share the task with them.

Adults in a Child's Life Today

Who will be the adults in their child's life? How will these adults influence their child? Bill and Jane know that these questions may be more critical than when to take parental leaves or which home to buy. They have planned child care and are scheduling "at home" time. But these plans may not balance the changed influence of adults in the child's life. They share the fears of many parents in their age group. No one knows how it is all going to turn out.

Adults will still be attached to children during the

nineties. The nature of that attachment, however, will be significantly different. The technological age and now the information age have brought with them a shift in human presence. "Human doing" is replacing "human being." An individual's worth relates more to function than to being. Both the "who" and the "what" of adults in children's lives have changed.

Parents

Of course, there will be parents. Yet the marital status of parents has changed. During the early nineties, an increased number of new parents will be single, never-married persons. Many second marriages will create blended families. What type of understanding of marriage will the children in these families develop? Parents have become "doers." Bill and Jane, like 90 percent of the parents of children today, will return home from work to *do*. They will *do* extra work-related projects, *do* food preparation, *do* laundry, *do* repair work, *do* yard work, *do* recreational activities, and whatever else the available time allows. The possibility of flexible hours may allow one parent's presence at home before and after school. But will there be other children in the neighborhood during daytime hours for playing? Will they have time as a family to enjoy playing games together? Or will they add to the twenty-five-year trend of a 40 percent decrease in time parents spend with a child?

Bill and Jane had planned to return to church when

they had their first child. They wonder if that time will be needed for routine shopping and leisure activities for their child and themselves. The child must take lessons—at least music, swimming, gymnastics, and computers. "Doing for" is a priority as parents seek to produce an improved child. Yet they want their child to learn Christian values. They heard a recent news report on the Search Institute's study on factors that promote faith maturity. Lifelong involvement in formal Christian education and family religiosity were at the top of the list. Perhaps they will need to review their priorities!

Relatives

Job relocation and new career options have distanced Bill and Jane from their relatives. Air travel has allowed annual holiday trips to visit their parents. Will this practice continue? The combined pressures of work and parenting will make a difference in how they use vacation time. They need to establish their own family traditions. Supporting a child will increase their household costs. Encouraging their parents to visit them may be the only answer. But with four grandparents employed full-time, they may need to plan joint vacations. Scheduled "doing" will replace spontaneous "being." Perhaps they can renew the relationship with Jane's father. He has freedom to visit them due to early retirement. Bill and Jane doubt that their child will experience interacting with cousins. Several divorces and remarriages among their siblings have complicated regular attendance at family reunions. Mailed cards and gifts will need to replace gathering in person for celebrations.

Child Care Workers

Child care workers will provide the most regular contact with other adults for Bill and Jane's child. These persons, predominantly females, vary in their training and experience in relating with children. Following carefully outlined standards, they are doing a job for pay. Will their child need to search for male role models as Jane did? Will these persons provide the loving atmosphere they want for their child? Although many of these workers develop a deep love for the children, the boundaries for expressing affection are carefully maintained. The community's Resource and Referral Service felt their concern for health, safety, and early education would be addressed through the standards maintained by a high quality center. They don't want to act as nonpresent parents who suspect abuse quickly. Assurance of a center's high standards will help reduce this anxiety.

Teachers in Public and Private Schools

In choosing a location for their new home, Bill and Jane will carefully examine the public school system and private educational opportunities. They can screen before-and-after-school caregivers, but they must depend on the school administration's selection of elementary teachers. They have heard rumors about teachers having so many assigned responsibilities that their highest priority is simply to survive day to day. Will these persons seek to cultivate nurturing relationships with their child? Or will they simply carry out a day's routine, doing what has to be done?

Neighbors

Bill and Jane know relationships with neighbors will be limited. Between double-income families and single-parent households, persons with children do not have time to engage in neighboring activities. "Neighbor" means only physical proximity today. "Cocooning" provides limited social interactions beyond the walls of one's own home. A neighbor's contact with the child will probably address an immediate need. Many never-married singles and childless couples live in areas where Bill and Jane looked for a home. They doubt that social activities with these adults will include their child. Perhaps they need to investigate the surrogate grandparent program advertised recently through their local paper. Or if they decide to return to church, their child might develop friendships with adults there.

The Media Adult

Bill and Jane have not identified one group of adults that will significantly influence their child. These adults are on the media screen in their own home and in the child-care center. From Saturday morning cartoons to the rented video movie, a variety of adults will connect with their child. These adults seek to do a great show. They need to keep ratings up, produce a commercial to generate sales to millions of people, or a "hot" video to stimulate video rental and sales. Someone's desire for money influences what the child sees on the screen. The potential of psychological abuse through a child's exposure to unfiltered information is not a priority concern for media producers. The media adults, mythical and real, will provide cues for learning the language of intimacy, definition of roles, and life-style standards.

The Changing Adult Influence in Children's Lives

Yes, Bill and Jane's child and other children of the nineties will attach to adults. The "who" has changed since their own childhood, but there are still adults around. It is the nature of that attachment and resulting influence that have changed drastically. The shift from "human being" to "human doing" has altered the environment. The child of the nineties will respond to new cues for cognitive, affective, and behavioral development. The influence of adult "doers" will interrupt the natural movement from dependence to independence to interdependence. Children will enter and stay in the sphere of independence too early in life. In this sphere of independence they will shape their own self-centered identities that may not integrate well into an adult world.

Despite the many changes, Bill and Jane have expectations for their first child that are similar to their own parents' expectations for them. They want their child to gain a sense of worth and purpose to live a meaningful life. Will the adult "doers" surrounding the child provide the needed stimulus for this development?

If Bill and Jane visit the church where Mr. Watkins serves as pastor, what opportunities will they have to gain understanding of their role as parents? To renew their own relationship with God? To connect their child with significant others? To expose their child to Christian teachings? Will they meet the Jemisons and share the joys and pains of parenting? Or Todd's parents, who can share the story of a growing faith during many years of painful waiting for his birth? Will they link with the O'Neills as surrogate grandparents? Or the Garcias, who serve as "aunt and uncle" for many?

For Bill and Jane, the Bradleys, the Reynoldses, the Andrews, and many other parents in the nineties, there is hope! That hope is the Christian community as manifested in a church with members who communicate faith through sharing knowledge and "being" in relationships. Caring Christians can help parents in developing the child's strong sense of identity. It cannot be bought in the marketplace, mailed from afar, scheduled in a child-care center, or watched on a media screen.

The church of the nineties must take seriously the task of aggressively seeking to be a partner with parents. It must become a primary source of instruction and support for both parent and child. It cannot be just another demand for time, energy, and money.

Parents and children need a core of persons deeply committed to family well-being to help them survive and thrive. The Christian community can provide these persons. They will be in churches whose leaders see a ministry with parents and children as a mission. They will believe a child's development is worth the investment of their time, talent, and resources—their entire being. The rest of this book speaks directly to these faithful human beings and others who may join them in ministry with children and their parents during the nineties.

III

The Christian Community's Mission with Children

Each year many persons receive do-it-yourself kits as gifts. The beginnings of a finished product are present. A gift like this was received by a friend a few years ago. The gift came complete with fabric, yarn, hoop, and needle. The recipient needed only to give time and effort to the project—to envision the end result and follow directions. Yet the recipient placed the kit in a drawer and left it there for five years. Finally, the friend gave the kit back to the giver for completion.

God's gift of children is like the gift of a kit. The basic parts come with the gift. But, like all kits, children need contact with persons who will give time and effort to the task of development. These persons must envision the end result and discern directions along the way. Unlike the needlework kit

41

noted above, those who receive children cannot set them aside and return them after a few years. They cannot depend totally on the Giver for the development task. God will help, but the Giver won't do it all.

Parents and church communities who receive children into their lives must give time and effort to their development. A parent must accept responsibility for the child's total growth—body, mind, and spirit. The church shares in fulfilling the responsibility for spiritual formation by establishing a partnership with the parent. The church serves in a support role. The parental influence, whether based on a Christian commitment or not, will be primary in this developmental process.

Both partners must answer the questions, What is the desired end result? and, What directions do we follow? For the Christian community, the desired end result is a fully functioning Christian. Good intentions, however, will not translate automatically into this end result. Specific directions must be identified. A mission must be discerned.

In the Christian community, the unfolding story of salvation throughout scripture provides the basis for each child to:

(1) restore an intimate relationship with God as revealed in the Son, Jesus Christ, and enabled by the Holy Spirit;

(2) understand the value and significance of each person as part of the whole;

42

(3) recognize that one is dependent on and incomplete without others; and

(4) accept the responsibility to care for all of God's creation.

Children must answer for themselves the questions: Who is God? Who am I? Who are you? How can I care for all of God's creation?

Who is God? Studying God's Word will provide foundational knowledge and experience through which the Holy Spirit will enable children to know God. However, God is more than an idea to be learned about. Children must have opportunities to know God in the Hebrew sense—to experience the omnipresent I AM. They need to develop spiritual disciplines to draw near to God. They need to learn the language and practice of worship.

Who am I? Through knowing God, the child will better understand his or her own value and significance. Faith will be personal and inform one's way of being in the world. The innate search for meaning will be a search for God's purpose and direction. When asked the question, "What do you want for yourself?" the child's response will reflect a self-sharing orientation, not a self-serving one.

Who are you? The child needs to develop relationships with others of varied ages, gender, physical and mental abilities, ethnicity, and lifestyles. Through these relationships, children will better understand their own value, significance, and incompleteness without others. Experiences with all ages will help the child link past, present, and future. Learning about and interacting with persons from other cultures will help develop the language of "we." Preparation will begin for interdependent living in a global community.

How can I care for all of God's creation? The child must develop a mutual relationship with all of creation. "Giving" needs to balance "taking." Living as responsible stewards, the children will seek to develop and use God's gifts for the Creator's purposes. The fully functioning Christian will live in harmony with the Creator and creation!

Discerning a Local Church's Mission with Children

One church cannot be everything to everyone! Those who attempt to be often find they are nothing for many. Each local church needs to discern its mission with children at a particular time, in a particular place, with the resources that God has provided. A mission statement for children's ministry will identify the local church's unique role within the larger Christian community. The mission statement will guide the processes of evaluating current activities, making appropriate choices for future programming, and determining needed resources.

Many persons need to provide input for developing a mission statement. The process provides an opportunity to develop commitment to and ownership of the mission. Children's ministry leaders must communicate the stated mission with potential partners. Information is needed by the entire congregation, parents, church governing bodies, community organizations, and governmental agencies. They need to know what the church is really trying to do and be with children.

An elected or appointed planning group should assume the specific responsibility of developing the mission statement. They will gather and analyze data, do visioning, and write a proposed mission statement for final approval by a larger governing body.

Basic questions must be asked and answered. For example:

What are the needs? the opportunities?
What are the current strengths?
What do we value? believe is important? see happening?

Identifying Needs and Opportunities

The local church's setting for ministry includes specific needs and opportunities for children's ministry. Persons both inside and outside the church should provide input through formal and informal means. A review of this data helps a group to find possible key result areas. After reviewing the current situation, the group needs to consider emerging trends in society. A summary article or visual showing trends should be available for group reflection. Questions at this point should include, What are

45

possible implications of these trends in our setting? and, What will be future needs and opportunities?

Identifying Strengths, Values, Beliefs

The group must reflect on current strengths. What things are being done well now? What resources has God supplied? Gathering reviews (formal and informal) from a broad base of attenders and nonattenders helps to avoid biased evaluations. Input from parents and children can help confirm others' perceptions.

Peter Drucker in *Managing a Non-profit Organization* states, "Do better what you already do well—if it's the right thing to do." Knowing the "right thing to do" requires identifying what is important to a group, their values, their beliefs. The answers to these questions will reflect the local church's biblical understandings and theological views. They will include an understanding of human development theories and the learning process.

Writing the Mission Statement

After identifying current strengths and "what's important here," the group must look for "matches." What needs and opportunities connect with current strengths? How do these relate to what we believe is important and should happen? The responses to these questions provide a basis for writing the mission statement.

For example, an inner-city church's planning

group for children's ministry summarized the basis for their mission statement as follows:

Needs: to decrease the crime rate among children; to support single parents in their parenting role
Opportunities: to network with persons outside the church through the day-care center
Current strengths: high quality day-care center operating 6:00 A.M. to 9:00 P.M., six days a week; well-trained, deeply committed staff; large endowment fund provided by a former member
Beliefs/values: God cares for the poor. God can serve as the protector and guide for lonely children. The church and parent must be partners. Christian growth can stop at-risk behaviors.

The church adopted a mission statement for their ministry with children as follows:

We will seek to serve children, birth through age twelve, of families within a twenty-mile radius of our church. We will provide experiences that enable each child to know the reality of God as protector and guide. We will provide opportunities for children to develop behaviors reflecting Christian values and a desire to serve others.

The worksheet on the following pages can help a planning group summarize the basic elements of a mission statement for their children's ministry.

Basic Elements of a Mission Statement for Children's Ministry

Directions: Within each of the areas given below, identify what you believe are essential elements for stating your church's mission with children. You may choose more than one in each section.

Given Our Context for Ministry:

Specific needs/Opportunities

____ children   _____

____ adults   _____

____ families   _____

____ community   _____

____ other _____   _____

And Strengths:

Current Programming   Available Resources

_____   _____

_____   _____

_____   _____

The Children's Ministry of _____ Church Shall Seek to Serve:

____ birth through age 12 (within church family)
____ birth through age 12 (within sphere of church contacts)
____ children, birth through age 12, and families (within church)
____ children, birth through age 12, and families (within sphere of church contacts)
____ other _____

Through Providing Opportunities for Developing Relationships With:

Needed Emphasis

_____ God   _____

_____ self   _____

_____ other persons   _____

_____ all of Creation   _____

In Coordination and Cooperation With:

_____ parents
_____ the larger congregation
_____ the church governing bodies (List:_____)
_____ schools (List:_____)
_____ community organizations (List:_____)
_____ government agencies (List:_____)
_____ other (List:_____)

Defining Programming to Accomplish the Mission

Tradition should not define children's programming. Nor should a search for "what works to get them there and keep them." The choice of programming relates to accomplishing the mission.

The mission statement is a filter for reviewing current programs. It helps leaders decide what to expand, what to continue as is, what to add, and what to discontinue. The key questions will be: Will this advance our capacity to carry out our mission with children? and, Do we have enough resources (human competence and commitment, finances, equipment, and facilities)? Discontinuing a program that contributes minimally to accomplishing the mission will allow redistribution of resources.

No standard listing of programs accomplishes a particular church's mission with children. The following list of programming options provides a stimulus for thinking, but it is not inclusive. Review the listing and ask the following questions: Which activities are now a part of our local church children's ministry? Which represent future possibilities? What could we add to the listing?

General
   Sunday school
   Promotion and Rally Sundays
   Sunday school picnic
   Parent and child events
Summer ministries
   Vacation Bible School
   Day camps
   Retreats
   One-day events
   Athletics and recreation
Creative arts
   Vocal and handbell choirs
   Music lessons
   Classes in puppetry, drama, art, etc.
Child care
   Nursery care on Sunday
   Weekday volunteer child care
   Full-day child care
   School-age child care
Nursery and preschool programs
   Weekday preschool programs
   Weekday clubs for preschool age

School-age programs
   Weekday clubs for elementary age
   Pastor and child interaction groups
Worship
   Children's sermon
   Children as greeters, ushers,
      and candlelighters
   Children's worship or church time
   Children's bulletins
Missions and stewardship
   Children's mission education program and
      projects
   Children's stewardship education program
Church year and holidays
   Church Year Celebrations (Advent, Christmas,
      Epiphany, Lent, Easter, Pentecost)
   Children's Day celebrations
   Alternative Halloween celebrations
   Thanksgiving celebrations
   Other holiday celebrations (as appropriate for
      the setting)
Special learning opportunities
   Children's library (printed materials, cassette
      tapes, and videos)
   Computer learning centers
   Orientation classes and visitors' packets for new
      children
   Children's newsletter
   Programs for those with disabilities

No one program stands alone to fulfill the church's mission with children. All are part of the whole to help children grow in their relationship with God, self, others, and all of creation. Coordination is essential to assure balance. Similarities and differences must be understood by staffs for various programs.

Persons planning the church's programming for children must understand the specific purpose of individual programs. Five general ministry goals can help planners identify the emphasis for each program. These include worship, study, fellowship, service, and evangelism.

The following worksheet can help groups summarize the emphasis of current programming for various age levels to guide future planning. This picture of the church's ministry with children will provide insights regarding areas that need more or less emphasis.

Identifying Emphases for Children's Programming

Directions: On the left side, list each aspect of your church's current children's programming. Use an X in the appropriate right columns to note your perception of each program's current emphasis. Remember, more than one can be checked.

Age Level: _____

Program	Worship	Study	Fellowship	Service	Evangelism
_____					
_____					
_____					
_____					
_____					
_____					

Developing commitment to the mission is a key to effective implementation. As noted before, the process of writing the mission statement helps create ownership and initiates movement toward commitment. Children's ministry leaders must help persons live out this commitment. They must provide adequate resources, training, and support.

The next section gives practical suggestions for assessing the teaching-learning processes, choosing curriculum materials, creating learning environments, and staffing for ministry. Attention to each area will enhance the probability of translating mission into ministry.

IV

Assessing the
Teaching-Learning Processes

The choice of programs for children's ministry and the identification of specific emphases for such programs represent a beginning step. Guidelines for the actual teaching-learning process need clarification. The subject matter, the teaching strategies, and the dynamics of teacher-student interaction must be considered.

Published curriculum materials are helpful in identifying subject matter and teaching strategies appropriate for an age level. Yet the choice and use of curriculum materials is only part of the task of promoting learning. The curriculum is more than written plans and materials. It includes the unwritten "happenings" initiated by children and teachers.

The following checklists provide a general listing of guidelines for assessing the teaching-learning process for various age levels. The use of these guidelines can help children's ministry leaders identify areas of strength to expand and areas for improvement to promote maximum learning.

Review each listing and indicate your perception of the current teaching-learning processes for each age level.

Assessing the Teaching-Learning Processes

Directions: Circle the number that best describes these experiences for the noted age level. Use the rating scale of 1—Excellent, 2—Good, 3—Needs some work, and 4—Needs serious thought.

(Age 2 and under as appropriate)

1 2 3 4 Stories are told in groups of four or less.

1 2 3 4 The Bible is open to the story and central as the teacher relates it.

1 2 3 4 Stories emphasize God's love and care, especially focusing on the child's present contact with creation.

1 2 3 4 Stories are simple, yet teach Bible truths.

1 2 3 4 Scripture words to be repeated are personal and meaningful with the child's name inserted.

1 2 3 4 Songs sung by the teacher convey easily understood Bible truths and scripture verses.

1 2 3 4 Concepts of God's goodness to the children are incorporated into conversation.

1 2 3 4 Simple prayers of praise and thanks are heard by the child.

1 2 3 4 Children are welcomed individually and their needs responded to individually.

(Ages 3 through 5)

1 2 3 4   Stories are told in groups of not more than twelve.

1 2 3 4   The Bible is open to the story and central as the teacher relates it.

1 2 3 4   Children help prepare the worship center and participate in worship.

1 2 3 4   Stories emphasize God's love and care, especially focusing on creation, patriarchs, Jesus, his resurrection, and disciples.

1 2 3 4   Songs reinforce easily understood Bible truths and scripture verses.

1 2 3 4   Scripture words to be repeated or memorized are meaningful to the children.

1 2 3 4   Concepts of God's goodness to them are naturally incorporated into conversation.

1 2 3 4   Prayers focus on praise and thanks, although "forgiveness" prayers may begin.

1 2 3 4   Children are known and welcomed individually and their needs responded to individually.

1 2 3 4   Children are encouraged to bring offerings and participate in "giving" projects for others.

(Grades 1 through 3)

1 2 3 4   Stories are told in groups of not more than twelve.

1 2 3 4   The Bible is open and central when the story is told.

1 2 3 4   Stories focus on God's love and promises for individuals and all people of the world.

1 2 3 4   Children are given a Bible of their own.

1 2 3 4   Children are helped to find the scripture story in the Bible.

1 2 3 4   Children are familiar with the parts of the Bible and can find them.

1 2 3 4   The order of worship is explained so children can follow it.

1 2 3 4   Familiar parts of worship are practiced such as the Doxology and the Lord's Prayer.

1 2 3 4   Participation in worship is encouraged through choir, drama, candlelighting.

1 2 3 4   Concepts of sin, Jesus' death and resurrection, and the coming of the Holy Spirit are introduced.

1 2 3 4   God's plan of salvation is sensitively presented as life's most important choice.

1 2 3 4   Opportunities for quietness are provided.

1 2 3 4   Prayer includes praise, thanks, confession, intercession, and petition.

1 2 3 4   Scripture promises and words of assurance are memorized.

1 2 3 4   Pros and cons of choices are discussed.

1 2 3 4   Small intergenerational groups are planned to encourage adult-child friendships.

1 2 3 4   Stewardship and mission opportunities are provided.

1 2 3 4   Children are known and welcomed individually and their needs responded to individually, if possible.

(Grades 4 through 6)

1 2 3 4 Stories are told in groups of not more than twelve.

1 2 3 4 The Bible is open and central when the story is told.

1 2 3 4 Stories focus on God's love and promises for individuals and all people of the world.

1 2 3 4 Children use a Bible of their own.

1 2 3 4 Children are familiar with the books of the Bible and can find Bible references.

1 2 3 4 Children learn how the Bible came to be.

1 2 3 4 Children begin to trace the story of God's people and the relationship of significant events/individuals to the whole.

1 2 3 4 Worship is experienced in a variety of settings.

1 2 3 4 The order of worship is explained, noting why we have various parts.

1 2 3 4 Familiar parts of worship are practiced, such as the Doxology and the Lord's Prayer.

1 2 3 4 Participation in worship is encouraged through choir, drama, candlelighting, reading of scripture.

1 2 3 4 Concepts of sin, forgiveness, Jesus' death and resurrection, and the coming of the Holy Spirit, discipleship, Christ's return, heaven, hell, death, are openly discussed.

1 2 3 4 God's plan of salvation is sensitively presented.

1 2 3 4 Opportunities for quietness are provided.

1 2 3 4 Prayer includes praise, thanks, confession, intercession, and petition.

1 2 3 4   Scripture promises and words of assurance are memorized, including passages of scripture and Psalms.

1 2 3 4   Small intergenerational groups are planned to encourage adult-child friendships.

1 2 3 4   Pros and cons of decisions are discussed.

1 2 3 4   Opportunities are available to explore abilities and gifts.

1 2 3 4   Stewardship and mission opportunities are provided.

1 2 3 4   A class is planned for older children on preparing for adolescence.

1 2 3 4   Children are known and welcomed individually and their needs responded to individually, as possible.

V

Choosing Curriculum Materials

The curriculum material provides a common reference point for those guiding the teaching-learning process. It sets priorities for concept formation. It guides a systematic, comprehensive exploration of a body of knowledge. It identifies desired content for particular age groups through goals and objectives. It pairs tested methodology with content, to encourage acquisition, application, and retention of knowledge and skills appropriate to a specific age level. It establishes guidelines for the evaluation process. It guides the development of a total learning environment.

The Sunday school curriculum materials can serve as the base for making curriculum decisions in other program areas. As Jack Seymour states in *Renewing the Sunday School and the CCD*, "the Sunday school has an exploratory, introductory, and foundational function on which more systematic and cumulative settings for study may be built." Sunday school is the setting in which children can learn the basics of the faith. Other programs can reinforce and expand these learnings. The choice of resources for children's worship, weekday activities, special summer events, and other specialized programs should complement and add to the Sunday school curriculum materials.

Developing comprehensive curriculum materials requires considerable time and persons with specialized knowledge and skill. Therefore, most churches depend on denominational or outside publishers to provide curriculum materials for their congregation. The cost of these materials represents a large percentage of most Christian education budgets. Good choices maximize this financial investment and advance the church's capacity to fulfill its stated mission with children. Guidelines for choosing materials should address the church's specific concerns for content, methodology, and usability.

The development of guidelines for choosing curriculum materials is a task in which the whole church has a stake. Yet a small group must do the initial work. The most informed, experienced parents, teachers, and church leaders, including the pastor, should propose guidelines. These should suit the character of the church and relate to fulfilling the stated mission. It also should reflect an understanding of what children need to know and become in order to mature in Christ. The process includes answering questions related to appropriate content, available leadership, leadership development, equipment and materials, desired learning activities, scheduling, and finances. The proposed guidelines should be submitted to the appropriate church governing body for approval. The broader the base for approval, the stronger the overall commitment will be to implementation.

Guidelines for Selecting Curriculum Materials

The following list can serve as a "starter" for groups developing guidelines to choose curriculum materials.

Step 1: Select the guidelines your church wants to use.

Step 2: Identify at least two curriculum materials to review.

Step 3: Rate them using the following scale: 0—Not at all; 1—OK; 2—Good; 3—Great!

CONTENT

_____ Opportunities are provided for the children to learn biblical stories and concepts appropriate to the age level targeted.

_____ Opportunities are provided for the children to learn the background and structure of the Bible.

_____ Opportunities are provided for the children to learn about past and contemporary heroes of the Christian faith.

_____ Opportunities are provided for the children to learn about:

____ Creation

____ Salvation

____ Holy Spirit

____ Prayer
____ Worship
____ Sacraments
____ Stewardship/Life-style
____ Mission (local, world, other)
____ Church year
____ Church music

____ Concepts, stories, and graphics are multiethnic and gender inclusive.

____ Contemporary family structures and interests of the age group are adequately considered and realistic.

METHODS

____ Clear, attainable objectives are provided for each session.

____ Alternative methods are suggested for presenting content.

____ Choices are given for reinforcement activities that recognize different learning styles.

____ Meaningful learner participation and involvement are encouraged.

____ Practical, realistic applications of the content are included in each session.

____ A variety of methods to memorize scripture are suggested.

AGE LEVEL ABILITIES

____ Suggestions are given for a broad range of abilities (two-year age range).

____ Simple to more in-depth opportunities for learning are allowed.

EVALUATION

____ Opportunities are provided to assess the learner's progress in acquiring desired knowledge, skills, and attitudes.

PREPARATION

____ Session material and format are easy to understand, prepare, and use.

____ Session plans allow for adjustable time frames for class length (30 minutes to 90 minutes)

____ Information is provided to help teachers and planners understand how individual sessions fit into the larger goals of the curriculum plan.

OUT OF CLASS INVOLVEMENT

____ Opportunities are provided for service and fellowship outside of class.

PARENT INVOLVEMENT AND PARENT EDUCATION

____ The partnership of church and home in supporting the child's spiritual growth is emphasized.

____ Parenting information for building effective relationships is provided in a variety of easy-to-use formats.

____ Opportunities are provided for parents to reinforce learning and spiritual development.

PUBLISHER SUPPORT FOR
LESSON IMPLEMENTATION

_____ Teacher aids are included to create a welcoming learning environment.

_____ Materials for specific lessons are included or easily accessed: video tapes, audio cassettes, song books.

PUBLISHER SUPPORT FOR
STAFF DEVELOPMENT

_____ Opportunities are provided for teachers to increase Bible knowledge and skill in using the Bible.

_____ Opportunities are provided for teachers to learn about characteristics of children, classroom management, and activities that match age and learning styles of children.

_____ Opportunities are provided for convenient and affordable training or consultation.

ENVIRONMENTAL IMPACT

_____ Minimum use of paper is required.

_____ Materials are concentrated so exact number needed can be generated "in house."

COST

_____ Options are offered for purchasing basic curriculum materials and adding supplements, rather than buying the "complete package" at one time (reduces costs and maximizes individualization).

Additional considerations in choosing curriculum materials are as follows. These are not to be rated, but simply checked for matching a church's philosophy or specific need.

____ Sessions center around a major concept. (Children can miss a session and still develop an understanding of the major concept.)

____ A grouping of sessions moves from simple to complex. (Children need to be regular attenders to participate in a meaningful way.)

____ Sessions are self-contained with a new concept weekly. (Regular attendance is not critical to meaningful participation.)

____ Implementation of session plans is not heavily dependent upon equipment such as VCR, projectors, copy machine, overhead, etc.

____ Suggestions are provided to expand session plans for use in other programs such as church time, weekday ministries, or retreats.

The concern for quality and convenience that characterizes our society today can create tension in the curriculum material selection process. On the one hand, there is the parent demanding quality learning experiences for a child, with in-depth exploration of content. On the other hand, there are teachers wanting curriculum materials that are "user friendly"—not difficult to comprehend or requiring a long preparation time. Those who guide the selection process must seek a "win-win" resolution of this conflict.

VI

Creating Learning Environments

A distinctive characteristic of young parents today is their insistence upon quality. They make great financial investments in food, clothing, cars, education, and homes to support this demand. Members and visitors come to church as SCAN-Rs. They note if the facility is S-afe, C-lean, A-ttractive, and N-eat; their assessment determines if they will R-eturn.

Churches need to recognize this concern for quality when creating or redesigning environments. Careful attention must be given to allocation of versatile space, equipment and materials, storage, quality assurances, and user-friendly status.

Allocation of Versatile Space

When allocating space, two major questions need to be answered: Who will use the space? and, How will the space be used?

Consideration for the age level and number of children in a group is vital in assigning space. To decide the needed size of an area for children, multiply the expected number of children by 30 to 35 square feet for young children (birth through 5 years) and by 25 to 30 square feet for older children (6 through 12 years). The product is the amount of square footage needed. Include storage space in your total amount.

There is a limit to the number of children that it is safe to have within a group, regardless of space. Professional credentialling groups provide recommendations for this optimal group size and the ratio of adults to children. Basically, the younger the child, the smaller the number in the group and the lower the adult-child ratio. For example, the recommended maximum number of eight-year-olds in a group is 24, with a 1 to 12 adult-child ratio. Infant groups have a maximum of 8, with a 1 to 4 ratio.

Using these guidelines to assess needed space, church leaders often discover that they are over-crowding children or have no room for growth. Creative thinking is essential! This will include restructuring age groups, changing schedule patterns of existing programs (such as having two Sunday schools), changing space assignments to maximize present facilities, or dividing large spaces in creative ways.

Children need lots of floor space, but large open spaces do not help them function well. They need visual and physical barriers to define boundaries and

69

the expected behavior. A place with many persons is overwhelming to children. Their heightened activity level or reluctance to participate is a good indicator of this.

Individualized areas created within a large space can accommodate attendance fluctuations, smaller age ranges, and smaller groups within an age group. Wide back-to-back movable shelves between 3½ and 4½ feet high are excellent dividers. They regroup the children within a space when strategically placed. These dividers provide good storage as well as visual barriers. Wall space, storage units, furniture, and free-standing storage displays can help create alcoves and places of focus scaled to the size of the child. These well-defined areas help children enjoy participation and enhance the teacher's ability to manage the activity of the group.

The nursery area should be a priority in assigning space for children's ministry today. The new parent will often assess the entire church on the merits of this area. It can be the number-one factor in a family's decision to return to the church. Additional information for designing a nursery is located in Appendix 1.

The second consideration in allocating space for children is the type of activities needed for effective ministry with different age groups. Programs that include recreational activities will need different space, room arrangement, and equipment than those used for worship or a church school class. A room that serves various types of programs must reflect consideration of each program's special needs.

For example, weekday child-care rooms get high use. The minimum health and safety standards required to maintain a license for such programs can complicate use by non-licensed groups. Staffs of the various programs need to realize that the sum of the programs builds a comprehensive children's ministry. This realization keeps these complications in perspective and enables better relationships between staffs of different programs.

The nursery is another area that serves a multi-program function. A posted room schedule may look as follows:

*Sunday A.M.:   Worship / S.S.   Infants (through 12 mo.)
*Tuesday A.M.: Women's Bible Study   Infants–5 years
*Thursday A.M.: Parent's Day Out   Infants (12-24 months)

Each program has different leaders. Each group needs different equipment, all within the same space. Sunday and Thursday take minor adjustments because of the limited age range. Child care for Tuesday's Bible Study is a different situation.

The use of portable mesh corrals and spring-tension gates can help churches resolve the issue of separate space for different ages and activities with young children. If there are more children in the upper early-childhood age groups (preschoolers) than in the toddler group, child care moves to a room with preschool-type equipment. Some toys, materials, and diapering supplies from the nursery accompany the caregiver. The very young are divided from the activities of the older ones to assure safety. If the majority of children present are younger, then some materials for the older children are moved to the nursery. The older children can spend some time in corrals playing with toys that they enjoy best without jeopardizing the safety of the toddlers.

Equipment and Materials

Furnishings used today should encourage comfort, aesthetics, sanitation, easy storage (stackable chairs and integrated cabinet systems), and flexible use (adjustable table-leg height, straight geometric lines). A valid concept to remember when equipping rooms for children is "less is better than more." Chairs and tables (especially round ones) within a room often take up valuable floor space.

Maximizing the use of equipment and modeling good stewardship require an "our" philosophy. Tables and chairs are the main items that different programs are willing to share. Beyond that, the predominant philosophy is "yours" and "mine." This can result in poor communication and a lack of appreciation for the use and storage of materials among the staffs of different programs.

For example, some weekday preschool programs strongly emphasize classification of materials. It is not unusual to find blocks stored on shelves, grouped by size. Leaders of other programs, who do not value the process of children sorting by size, may allow children to stow the blocks randomly. When the teachers in the weekday program return, they need to resort the blocks to prepare the environment. This takes time that could be used for other purposes. Thus, use of the same facilities by different groups can lead to continued misunderstanding.

When certain materials are special for a particular program, they should be stored in a secure, labeled place. Participants in each program need to respect the property of all others. "First aid" report cards for damaged or missing materials also enhance communication, understanding, and respect. The program leader in charge is responsible for contacting the age-level liaison to find possible replacement.

Creative use of walls and displays helps develop an "our" philosophy. Bulletin boards can be hung from hooks or pegs and reversed for another program's needs. Free-standing display boards of tri-wall, foam board, or oversized boxes provide display area. When collapsed flat, they are easy to store. Clotheslines strung at least 6 feet high, either against a wall or across a space, give additional area for display. These, too, are removed easily.

Storage

When planning an environment for children's ministry, adequate storage is very important. Good storage is accessible (close to where it is to be used); flexible (adapts to different sized equipment and materials); well organized (labeled shelves and containers allow convenient placement in relation to use); and secure (items stored in separate, closed containers or locked in some manner).

Each program's staff needs one person designated to assume the responsibility of seeing that the room is in order for the next group. If one program immediately follows another, the pickup can be part of the transition from one activity to another. Children need involvement in the clean-up and care of the environment with the adults.

An excellent way to provide storage and promote stewardship is through a central resource area that serves all programs. This area can be as small as a cart or as large as a room. A central resource center allows bulk purchase of supplies to reduce costs. It provides an area where the entire congregation can contribute recycled items. It creates better accessibility and accountability for use of materials and equipment.

Resource centers can be the storage center for:

* bulk supplies of consumables such as paper, crayons, pencils, and glue;
* recycled items such as frozen juice cans, paper-towel rolls, and yarn;
* special visual aids such as seashells, Advent wreaths, and costumes;
* old curriculum, pictures, or workbook activities, filed by theme for future use;
* audiovisuals such as filmstrips, films, videos;
* audiovisual equipment;
* maps, charts, and posters;

* flannel boards, chalk boards, and easels;
* teacher resource books;
* materials to make or preserve two-dimensional visual aids;
* resource books for children's use, such as dictionaries and atlases.

A resource coordinator, volunteer or paid, is essential to maximize effective use of this area. The coordinator receives requests for equipment and material from the program staff. This person then fills the orders and makes the supplies available in a special container for pickup or delivery.

A self-serve system can also be effective. A coordinator can be present to respond to questions and assume replacement responsibilities. Because of time pressure, it is often difficult for program leaders to "put things back" immediately.

Quality Assurances

Many professions and products have standards of excellence. Environments for children are no exception. Standards and policies provide some level of assurance that the place is safe for all who are there. Informing and training staff, parents, and children of these policies is a critical aspect of assurance. Churches are accountable for the safety of persons on the premises or at sponsored events. Documentation of high standards provides a significant measure of quality assurance for persons, irrespective of the program. Churches should take basic steps of risk management when providing for the physical care and education of children. These include:

* adhering to high standards in the maintenance of facilities;
* maintaining group size and child-adult ratios established by licensing agencies for the age group;
* screening staff, both paid and volunteer, during recruitment;
* developing and communicating policies and procedures for the care and security of children (e.g., bathroom procedures, buddy systems, transportation guidelines, behavior problems, and discipline);
* training staff in first aid and related health precautions;
* providing staff with information about child-abuse prevention and allegations;
* providing staff with information on insurance coverage and the consequences of "negligent" behaviors.

User-Friendly Environment

Many factors influence the creation of a "user-friendly" environment. Three key indicators are accessibility, attractiveness, and affective climate.

Accessibility. Realtors and church developers proclaim, "Location, location, location." This is true also in designating areas for children's ministry. When deciding room assignments, try to group similar ages together. Consider the proximity of bathroom and water sources. Note stairways and exit doors. Appendix 1 provides specific suggestions for the nursery area.

The pathways to children's areas should draw a person there. Signs, arrows, color, and special symbols help both children and parents find their way upon entering a building. Appropriate art work along a corridor indicates an area where one will find children. While a self-service environment is helpful, it can never replace greeters strategically placed throughout the building. The personal welcome says, "This is a place where caring for people is a priority."

Attractiveness. Most persons, especially visitors, note quickly "how good a room looks." Coordination is essential for attractiveness. Visual stimuli set a tone for activity in the room. Earth tones give a sense of warmth. Keep floors and walls a neutral color. Brighter colors "splashed" through decorations can draw the eyes and the emotions to areas of focus.

In some rooms or spaces, children's work and decorations cover nearly every inch of wall and ceiling space. There is no point of focus or a "neutral zone" that provides rest for the eyes. Spaces with clear focal points for both high energy and calmness provide for meaningful engagement. They also help to encourage self-control.

Floor surfaces can attract or detract! Carpeting helps to absorb sound, is comfortable for sitting on, and provides a warm feeling to the room. Intense colors, large patterns, and loose shag are poor carpet choices. Spaces with vinyl or wood flooring can be partially carpeted, with the carpeted area designating the gathering place. Area rugs, no matter how large, need to be securely attached to the floor.

Natural light is very desirable. Opportunities to regulate the intensity of light, both natural and artificial, are beneficial. The intensity of light can serve as a cue for behavior such as resting, sleeping, reading, or playing.

Affective Climate. While attractiveness can be an immediate draw to a location, it will not sustain continued participation and attendance. Personalized attention to the individual is essential. Persons involved with children's ministry must invest time in knowing who the children are, where they live, and their interests. Updated enrollment/information cards are a useful tool for getting to know children outside the church setting. Contacts through visits, telephone calls, and written communications to recognize their celebrations, accomplishments, and disappointments can convey real caring.

Greeters, both adults and children, must show genuine interest in and welcome toward whoever arrives. Name tags for adults and children say, "I want you to know my name," "I want to know yours," and "I want you to know the others who are here." Both visitors and regular group members have a responsibility in establishing relationships.

Families who visit appreciate an efficient procedure that gathers the minimum necessary information on their children. First, it shows parents that the church wants to know about the child to incorporate the individual into the program. Second, it shows that the church provides a high quality program that recognizes health, safety, and security standards. Inquiring about the names of child and parents, the child's age, special health needs, a parent's location, and who can pick up the child indicates a well-run program. Third, such a procedure acknowledges the parent's high interest in the child's well-being in spite of the limited time.

A new visitor packet for children can be very helpful to both child and parent. This packet includes an instant photograph of the child and basic information regarding the programs for the family and how the child may participate. An orientation session can help children understand the program and learn what to expect. Follow-up cards sent by children and teachers can help the new child and parents feel welcome.

With the increased concern for teaching content today, children's ministry leaders must recognize the unintended content that is "caught" in the dynamics of the learning environment. It can either enhance or block learning. And, it will make a difference as to whether parent and child return!

The checklist on the following two pages identifies general criteria for church leaders to use in evaluating learning environments for different age groups. Add, revise, or delete items to address a specific situation.

Assessing the Learning Environment

Directions: Indicate the number that best describes the learning environment for children in your church using the rating scale of 1—Excellent, 2—Good, 3—Needs some work, and 4—Needs serious thought.

All Ages

SPACE:

_____ The room size meets minimum standards for the age level.

_____ The group size does not exceed standards for the maximum number at the age level.

_____ The adult-child ratio does not exceed minimum standard for the age level.

_____ The room is appropriately child-proofed to assure safety.

_____ The room arrangement and decor create a general feeling of well-being.

_____ Floor plans are posted for each program to rearrange the room.

_____ A separated area for calmness and rest is available.

EQUIPMENT AND MATERIALS:

_____ Equipment and materials match the ability and interest of the ages served.

_____ There is clear understanding between "your" materials and "ours."

STORAGE:

_____ Adequate storage is available to assure a neat, organized appearance.

_____ A personal container/storage compartment is available for children's belongings.

USER FRIENDLY:

_____ The room is attractively decorated and provides areas of focus.

_____ The room is well lighted.

_____ The room is well ventilated.

_____ Appropriate visuals direct persons to the room.

_____ Most pictures and special displays are at the child's eye level.

_____ Children are encouraged to help in the maintenance of the room.

_____ Children are helped in establishing and maintaining guidelines regarding behavior in the room.

_____ Greeters are used to welcome children to the room.

_____ An efficient procedure is used to record essential information regarding a child and parent to assure appropriate care.

_____ Appropriate introduction to the group's activities is provided for each visitor.

VII

Staffing for Ministry with Children

It was the first Sunday in August. Two families stood before the congregation to receive their farewell gift. Four adults and six children would move to new locations in the next week. Three of the adults were involved in the church's children's ministry—the kindergarten Sunday school teacher, the children's choir director, and the fifth-sixth grade weekday club leader. The other adult was the Sunday school superintendent.

Where were the persons who would fill these positions? There were still gaps in staffing other programs. After many phone calls, letters, public pleas, and personal visits, the recruitment committee for children's ministry had a long list of unfilled positions. The need appeared to exceed the supply! The responses this year were different from those of previous years. There had always been nos, but the persons declining this year seemed to have different reasons. Where were the "faithful few"? What were the barriers to volunteer involvement? Could they meet the challenge of breaking through these barriers?

Persons responsible for recruiting children's ministry staff do have new challenges in the nineties. The total number of potential volunteers in the high-involvement group (ages 45-55) has declined. An older and younger majority is emerging. Routine household duties and leisure activities exhaust the discretionary time. A concern for personal growth and satisfaction motivates persons who say yes. "Getting a return on the investment" is essential. Supporting the church's ministry is no longer a tradition. An attitude that service is an option prevails. The call for excellence in the workplace shapes expectations for church ministry. Persons with limited church background decline service opportunities until they gain appropriate knowledge and skills. They will pay for the services of a professional to assure that the job is done and done well!

To meet these challenges, the church's governing body and those specifically responsible for planning and implementing a children's ministry must:

* envision new sources of potential volunteers;
* clearly articulate the church's mission with children;
* develop new opportunities for involvement in children's ministry;

83

* establish recruitment of children's ministry staff as a top priority;
* address liability issues through screening volunteers and providing adequate orientation for health and safety standards;
* plan for variety, practicality, quality, and convenience in orientation and training opportunities;
* personalize support and evaluation to meet the needs of individual volunteers; and
* be willing to commit monies to hire children's ministry staff as needed.

Envisioning New Sources of Volunteers. The growing number of older adults in congregations is a valuable source for staffing children's programs. Although retirement traditionally included disengagement from service commitments within the church, a shift in attitude and action is occurring. Older persons are choosing to stay involved! Distanced from their own grandchildren, they are discovering the joys and satisfactions of grandparenting as they minister to children and let children minister to them. Yet, they want freedom to be absent for short or long periods. They need short-term commitments and specialized roles to use their unique gifts.

Another potential source of volunteers is the young adult population (both married and unmarried without children). In contrast to the age group that precedes them, they are not highly motivated to acquire more in a material sense. They want more and more meaningful experiences. Cultivating relationships with children provides an opportunity to meet this need. Noted for being church shoppers, however, these volunteers must renew their commitment to the church and its ministry week to week!

A third source of volunteers is the group of older, mature senior highers displaying leadership potential. These youth surpass their elders in total hours of voluntary service. The primary emphasis of youth in mission has been cross-cultural experiences. Yet, older youth and their leaders are discovering that mission does not require "crossing the border or going to the inner city." Ministry with children in their own local churches and communities provides opportunities to express their faith. They gain ministry skills and basic knowledge to prepare for future parenting roles.

Parents do not represent a new source of potential volunteers. Yet recruiters must view their involvement in new ways. Parent-as-educator programs in public schools have created a new scenario. Parents are increasingly open to involvement and proving to be effective participants in the teaching-learning process. The child learns, and the parent gains knowledge and skills to function effectively in the parenting role. Church leaders must see this new scenario with parents as a prelude to expanded parent involvement in the church's ministry with children.

Tradition places persons aged 45-55 first on the list of potential volunteers. No new source is here! Yet a new understanding of these persons must characterize efforts to recruit and develop staff from this group. The majority, both male and female, are employed full-time. Many commit a large quantity of their discretionary time to caring for their parents. As a group, they display a deep need to search for meaning during this "slow down and stabilize" period. For most, the years of active parenting are past. The results have varied. They wonder, "Can we make a greater difference with this new generation of children?"

Common needs characterize these potential volunteers. Each group wants involvement that promotes personal growth and satisfies an inner need for meaning. They want the time investment to make a difference. They seek new opportunities for service to fit their available time. They need to serve in areas that tap their expertise and interests. They want practical orientation and training. They require individualized support and evaluation. They need relationships. They want to join a team!

Articulating the Church's Mission. Many persons today struggle with an inner hunger for congruency between personal effectiveness and growing relationships with other people. The search for a meaningful existence includes a search to connect with a "believable cause." The cause becomes so much a part of the volunteer's life that it satisfies personal needs related to reasons for being. It is at this point that the church can be very hopeful in its process of recruiting volunteers. The church has a believable cause! But the church's believable cause, its mission, must be clearly communicated to enlist the support of others. Potential volunteers are searching for the group or organization that knows where it is going.

Creating New Opportunities for Service. Service is not an option for the Christian! It is a way of living. Yet the choice of area, type of position, time involved, and energy expended are optional. Calling new volunteers into ministry requires removing the barrier of limited choices. Persons of varied ages and gifts must be joined together as a staff team. A team approach will allow persons to experience community and discover knowledge and skills together. The team must be large enough to encourage one-on-one relationship-building with children. Team members should function in their area of interest and skill. Each member should have regular time off without breaking leadership continuity with the children.

Persons recruited as greeters can welcome children and incorporate visitors into the group. Persons with experience in relating to those with disabilities can provide one-on-one assistance to children with special needs. Males should be encouraged to serve on staff teams for younger children. Older adults need to reenter ministry with children. Persons who want "at home" activities can serve in record-keeping positions and arranging followup with absentees and visitors. One-time or periodic involvement of persons with specialized gifts in the creative arts should be encouraged. And the list continues. It is limited only by the imagination of the planner and the gifts of potential volunteers.

Establishing Children's Ministry as a Priority. Church governing bodies and ministers need to prioritize children's ministry at the top of their list among many areas of concern. People respond to what others view as important. Children's ministry must be a primary area for investment of time, effort, and financial resources. In such churches, the choice of a qualified person for the kindergarten team will be made before the choice of persons for other ministries. The church will recognize its opportunity to shape an entire lifetime through ministry with a kindergarten child.

Addressing Liability Issues. A priority concern for the nineties is helping churches to be safer places for children. Screening potential volunteers who will interact with children is essential. Recruiters should review the volunteer's experience with children for evidence of nonabusive interactions and absence of negligence. One-on-one discussions with potential volunteers should confirm appropriateness of views related to supervision, discipline, and privacy rights.

Potential volunteers also express liability concerns. They ask, "What risks do I take when I say yes?" Although there are no 100 percent guarantees, the congregation can be proactive. Giving adequate attention to the following areas enhances the protection of persons involved with children's ministry:

(1) providing physically safe and secure environments;

(2) orienting volunteer and professional staff about security procedures and transportation of children to and from events;

(3) training children's ministry staff in the areas of first aid, CPR, disease control, or other health-related issues; and

(4) providing information for all children's ministry staff regarding discipline guidelines, physical contact with children, and adequate supervision.

Planning for Orientation and Training Opportunities. The Search Institute's 1990 report, *Effective Christian Education,* identified lifelong involvement in effective Christian education as vital to faith maturity. The use of the word *effective* implies that the church's educational ministry has a desired end result. The nature of that end result with children was discussed in chapter 3. Effective Christian education also implies a level of performance. In relation to performance, the study found that what matters is how well things are done, not how many things are done. "How well things are done" relates to quality orientation and training experiences.

The planners of preservice and inservice growth opportunities must address the individual needs of participants. Adult volunteers can be characterized in the five following ways, which can serve as a basis for designing orientation and training experiences.

1. Adults have knowledge and skills from their own secular work. In this setting they move from the known to the unknown. Youths have untested knowledge and skills. Fear may block learning. They need to know the goals and objectives for a specific program.

2. Adults and youth are impatient with extras. Time is a precious commodity. Their experiences in orientation must meet their expectations for quality, relevance, practicality, and convenience. First impressions determine their willingness to explore further training opportunities.

3. Previous teaching experiences with children provide some adults with habits. Childhood habits persist in older youth. Unfreezing present habits or memories, replacing them with a new habit, and refreezing the new habit requires frequent reward and reinforcement. People want "instant feedback" on how they are doing.

4. All persons will be at different levels of spiritual maturity. Their understanding and commitment to sharing the gospel with children will vary. Many young volunteers seek the "what and why" of the church's beliefs and traditions. They want input to stimulate their own faith formation.

5. Each person has a unique learning style. Some are thinkers—they simply want lectures and handouts to read. Others are "hands-on," action-oriented persons wanting a mini-lab school experience. A third type learns most through remembering their own childhood experiences, discussing with others, and discovering new learnings. A fourth type responds to the latest research and newest methodology, wanting always to "chase after the distant." Effective orientation and training will address each type.

Orientation begins during the recruitment process with the outlining of a job description and supporting resources. Preservice training can include group sessions, one-on-one meetings with an experienced leader, policy and procedure handbooks, or self-use audiovisuals. With the prevalence of home video cameras today, filming a basic orientation video for each task within the children's programming is possible. Having these videos available in a media library for individual checkout meets the volunteer's need for convenience. The availability of instant orientation via video helps incorporate new volunteers throughout the year.

Inservice training opportunities can include:

* team-building experiences
* teaming with a master teacher/leader
* one-on-one sessions between a beginner and experienced staff person
* regular staff meetings that include training "bytes"
* periodic staff planning to prepare for the next unit or series of sessions
* weekend retreats with guest resource persons
* regional workshops sponsored by the denomination or parachurch organizations
* a library with videos and programmed training sessions for individual use
* circulation of current periodicals, regular newsletters, and other written resources focusing on children's ministry

91

Persons responsible for designing orientation and training opportunities must answer these questions: Does it respect who is to be oriented or trained? Are choices available? Do the choices address the volunteer's need for personal growth? Do the experiences meet expectations for quality, practicality, and convenience?

Personalized Support and Evaluation. Individualization is the key to effective support. Recognition and support activities must consider personal needs. Younger volunteers want recognition for their specific contributions. They are often intolerant of impersonal group experiences. The young parent wants the whole family included in appreciation activities. Married persons want acknowledgment of the supportive spouse. Scheduling must consider the volunteer's time availability. Facilitating the development of relationships with other volunteers encourages cooperation and loyalty. Remember, isolation is the enemy of effective ministry.

Today's volunteers want to know where they stand—even if the news is not good. They want to know if they are doing a good job and helping to fulfill the church's mission. They also want to know if they are doing a poor job. They will seek help or consider alternative areas of service.

A major barrier to providing helpful feedback for those involved in children's ministry is the absence of written guidelines. Yet, unwritten expectations are ever present. After all, doesn't everyone know what effectiveness with children means? Those who depend on unwritten guidelines will soon find that "everyone" is actually "no one."

The following checklist is a beginning step in writing guidelines to provide feedback for persons involved with children's ministry. The checklist can be used individually by volunteers, with another person, or in a group.

Guidelines for Staff Effectiveness in Children's Ministry

_____ Staff understand goals and objectives for this area of ministry.

_____ Staff are empathetic, responsive, and consistently there when scheduled.

_____ Staff members affirm they are children of God.

_____ Staff members feel good about themselves and their part in this area of children's ministry.

_____ Staff are willing to pray specifically for each child and family represented in the room.

_____ Staff know a variety of techniques for interacting with children and managing groups of children.

_____ Staff are willing to learn more about this age level and additional ways to relate to these children.

_____ Staff support and value the contributions of other members of the child's family.

_____ Staff responsibly prepare for sessions.

_____ Staff participate in the lives of these children outside the church environment.

Committing Monies for Staff. When does the church hire staff to guide the ministry with children or a specific area of programming? What type of position should it be? One can respond by simply saying, "It depends." Each local church should evaluate its need for paid staff by using a checklist as follows:

_____ The need for recruiting, training, and supporting the volunteers involved in children's programs surpasses what can be provided by a volunteer within our congregation.

_____ The knowledge required for developing and maintaining the church as a safe place for children surpasses that available through volunteer leaders.

_____ The time needed for counseling with the families of children within the congregation and/or community surpasses what can be expected of the pastor or pastoral staff.

_____ The congregation voted to expand its ministry with children during the next five years.

A "yes" response to any item in the above listing indicates that the church needs to consider adding a paid staff person. The status of that position (full or part-time) relates to the time required for fulfilling the responsibilities. Needs determine the responsibilities. The nature of the specific tasks helps identify the qualifications of potential candidates. Possible positions include a children's ministry secretary, resource coordinator, nursery coordinator, early childhood coordinator, child-care coordinator, children's ministry coordinator, minister to children, and minister to families with children.

There is an increasing need in the nineties for persons with specialized training as ministers to children and families. Most of the persons now serving in these positions are female. However, more males are affirming a calling to children's ministry.

Denominational offices, seminaries, and local churches need to affirm ministry with children and their families as a vital context for evangelism and nurture. They must develop ways to encourage both males and females to consider this area of ministry as a lifetime calling. It should not be a "stepping stone" to "real" ministry. If that reorientation occurs, the church's children's ministry will begin to thrive, not just survive.

VIII

Becoming a
Family Resource Center

Bill and Jane, the expectant parents in chapter 2, are not currently active members of a church. In church involvement after the child is born, they join many of their peers returning to church as they begin to raise children. If Reverend Watkins and the congregation want to reach Bill and Jane, they need to be clear in discerning their mission with children and parents.

No church can "do it all." Effective ministry cannot take place in isolation. It happens in relationship. The mission statement developed in chapter 3 recognizes that implementation takes place in coordination and cooperation with other persons and groups. They create partnerships that can move from simple to complex.

Partnerships with Parents

The most critical partnership created in children's ministry is between the home and the church. Churches can meet their responsibility to parents by developing awareness of parental influence, equipping parents in their responsibilities, and extending support to families through various partnerships.

The Reverend Watkins' congregation is on target to attract new families. Parenting education will raise new levels of awareness regarding various aspects of parenting. Parent-education programs provide guidance for the physical care of children, expectations in child development, and effective ways to guide learning and behavior that will enhance family life.

Parents must recognize that they are the primary influences in the lives of their children. They are the ones who teach them how to live. They inform children of their worth.

Parents are the ones who socialize their children into acceptable behavior. Children assimilate information in the daily living and observing in the household. Children take on the mannerisms of their parents. Parents need to discipline themselves to speak and act the way they want their children to behave. They will discover that this is the most effective way for children to learn acceptable behavior.

Parents are interpreters of the world to their children. They are the ones who take the experiences of life and frame them in the context of deep underlying values. According to Lucy Barber, more than 50 percent of a child's values and attitudes toward life are in place by the age of three.

Parents are the creators of dependable environments for their children. They are the people who enable their children to learn to trust. They are the ones who can encourage hope. By creating a happy family life, they establish a place where forgiveness is experienced and love is known.

Equipping Parents in Their Responsibilities

Churches must clearly articulate what they believe. Families who attend church expect strong biblical teaching. Either they want to "make up for lost time" or seek more in-depth knowledge of scripture. The church needs also to provide meaningful worship. The pulpit ministry is part of the teaching ministry of the church. Adult class options should include amplification of the sermon themes as well as practical application to life's relationships. The church should provide materials expressing the beliefs of the local church. A strong adult education program needs to complement a strong children's program, including nursery. Attractive environments with friendly, knowledgeable teachers is not enough. Information shared must reinforce learning at home.

The language of commitment, love, and trust is foreign to many young parents. They leave the old behind in search of the new "best" in clothes, cars, jobs, homes, and mates. The church can help them learn the language of commitment through focus on the themes of loyalty and constancy found in the biblical story. Opportunities for marriage enrichment, parenting/grandparenting seminars, family life retreats, and intergenerational activities encourage building and strengthening relationships within the church and the extended family of origin. The creating and sharing of powerful memories in these events are vital to the process of establishing loyalty in both home and church.

Increasing parents' skill in passing their own faith stories to their children will have a long-term effect. Families ask for help with family devotions. They want to have positive times for sharing God's presence in their lives. Even when they are willing to make this time a priority, they may discover that the material offered does not match family interest.

One of the best opportunities for beginning a formal family devotional time is during Advent. The content and experiences appeal to all ages. Activities with Advent candles, special food, home decorations, and familiar stories are celebrative. Family members recall past shared experiences and create moments for new memories in the context of God's love. These key features enable success for future devotional times.

Churches can resource families in the area of service. Search Institute reports that helping others is a strong predictor of continued faith maturity. Families can work together on many projects such as collecting or preparing food for others, picking up trash at a park or near the church, caring for another's child, or adopting a grandparent. Younger children should be included. These years are a prime time to nurture care for others. It is often in simple, personal tasks that child and parent discover the joy of co-ministry.

While cooperative acts of kindness are very important, they do not take the place of church attendance and specific involvement. Children intuitively realize that if the adult commits time to something, it must be important. When parents are in Sunday school, children are there, too. When parents worship and assist children in worship, children will worship. It is likely that young families returning to church following the birth of their baby will not attend regularly. Churches need to be patient and ready to welcome them no matter what their decision. Appendix 2 includes more information on this subject.

Parents need meaningful inclusion in children's ministry. This participation usually begins with one-way communication. Then they attend special events. Next they help in some direct aspect of the program with their child. Some parents seek involvement with longer time commitments. They will lead groups of children or serve on a decision-making committee or board.

Parents have different levels of willingness and ability to become involved. A wise church recognizes this fact. It moves beyond a prescribed list of standard expectations. It develops a format that invites participation and friendship, utilizing a variety of options.

Parent involvement includes:

* reading materials sent from the child's class,
* attending special Parent's Day recognitions,
* visiting the child's class,
* encouraging friendships outside of the child's class,
* participating in church-home visits with the teacher,
* praying for the staff members and children at home,
* providing extra hands during an activity,
* helping with transportation to an event,
* serving as family greeters,
* attending workshops or borrowing resources to help in child rearing
* participating on an age-level advisory committee

Ray Oldenburg, in his book *The Great Good Place,* describes the human need for a place to simply "be." Oldenburg states that each person has three places today—a place where one lives, a place where one works, and a place where one relates (where you are known for who you are). The church needs to become the "great good place" for families. Church can be the place where people feel they belong. It is the place that encourages persons to balance the being and doing in life. It is the place where people can find meaning in life.

Children are born into and live within varying family structures. Within these structures, varying situations can arise. The list can be extensive. It may be the need for economic help which is lived out in housing, rent, and utility subsidies. It may be food, shelter, health care, or employment. There may be a need for mental health services or physical therapy for a family member with disabilities, or a need for a specific kind of child care. In each of these situations and many more, the church needs to offer some level of support.

Partnerships Within the Church

The "Basic Elements of a Mission Statement" worksheet provided in chapter 3 helps church leaders of children's ministry recognize that ministry does not happen alone. There is a need to link with their church governing bodies and other outside groups to provide coordinated support services for families. The church can become a viable family resource center. It can offer varying levels of intentional support to families with specific needs.

Possible Parenting Program Options

Moms and Muffins / Dads and Donuts

An informal support group with an attractive name. It encourages socializing, special speakers, discussions, creative projects, parenting skills, and other interests as the group determines. The child is in the nursery while the parent is in the meeting.

Mothers' Coffee

A regular social event for nurture and outreach to young mothers. Special attention is given to refreshments and decorations. Meetings include a Christian speaker, an area for books and tapes (either to borrow or purchase), and child care with planned learning activities.

Bible Studies

Prepared lessons on relational themes or specific books of the Bible from a parachurch organization or other source. Child care includes planned learning activities.

Denominational Men's and Women's Groups

Groups usually organized around common time available with focus on friendship, special service projects, and study materials.

Stay and Play

A child-guidance program for infants, toddlers, and parents. The parent spends time in class playing with the child and informally participates in parenting instruction on a variety of topics and techniques.

Vacation Church School for Preschoolers and Parents

Targets the summer program to a specific age group. Maintains intentional content links between both ages. Parents have some sessions separately with parenting topics.

Family Leisure Groups

Intergenerational events are planned in a special location and for an extended time frame. These groups encourage friendship, perform service projects, and develop ways to increase commitment to one another. Some locations include retreat, camp, and vacation sites.

Counseling

Uses members of the congregation who are legal, social services, medical, and mental-health professionals to provide help in such areas as: infertility, adoption, crisis pregnancy, foster care, grief, children with disabilities, spouse or child abuse, co-dependency and addictions.

Parent Support Groups

Support groups organized through the church for helping parents deal with specific issues. It may include a telephone hotline.

Possible Child Care Program Options

Using Volunteer or Paid Staff:

Nursery Service

Drop-off care for programs throughout the week such as worship, Sunday school, and choir rehearsal. No reservations or fee required.

Parent Child-Care Room

Care by child's parent in a room with a window adjacent to the sanctuary.

Child Care Cooperative

Child care in homes on an "as need" basis. No money is exchanged. Services are traded among a pool of people. Ledger sheets are kept to record points earned and used.

Weekday Care with Paid Staff and Pre-set Fees:

Coordinated Child Care (for church-sponsored activities)

Offered at the church for weekday programming. Reservations needed. Provides a consistent staff for developing relationships with children and for providing consistent expectations regarding behavior and use and care of the room. Especially helpful for churches with an active calendar and many young children whose parents are often at church. Reservations suggested. Fee to parent optional. Cost may be part of a specific ministry budget.

Parents Day Out

A weekly child care program from mid-morning through mid-afternoon for children 1 through 5 years (or younger). During summer older ages may be included. Reservations are required. Children bring lunch. It may need to be licensed by an agency.

Child Care in Homes

Child care programs offered in homes of church members. Homes must be licensed by the state and meet any special church requirements. A staff person could supervise and coordinate this ministry. The ages are mixed, and hours are more flexible than center based programs.

Licensed Child Care and Education

Full day and half-day programs for children housed in the church or other nonresidential building. It can serve the educational and care needs of children from the age of two weeks to twelve years. Some specialize in a specific age group such as infant-toddlers, preschool, or school age, including before and after school care.

Licensed Intergenerational Care

Full day or part-day programs for children and older adults within the church building or in a nursing home facility. The age groups are separate for part of the time and join together for certain activities. It provides a positive, realistic portrayal of aging for young children. Those in elder care contribute meaningfully to the new generation.

Partnerships with Community Resources

The prior listings are possibilities within a church's vision for mission. Child care may be staffed by church members. Some churches contract with an outside group to provide this weekday child-care service on behalf of the church. Some churches have the resources to provide for elemental family needs (for example, employment; housing, rent, and utility subsidies; emergency shelter, and a food pantry). However, when the needs move to economic survival, few churches are equipped to provide the full range of services. This is when limited or full partnerships need to develop between churches and geographic communities.

Limited partnerships can focus on the use of meeting space. Churches can be effective sponsors of such self-help and support programs for parents as Parents Anonymous, Compassionate Friends, and

Mother-to-Mother Ministry. Churches can open their doors to community health services to provide health and developmental screenings of children, immunization clinics, and nutritional feeding programs. In addition, some churches have their facilities used by publicly funded programs such as Head Start, a national compensatory preschool program for low-income children.

More and more preschool age children are identified as having special needs. This is partially the result of better procedures to sustain the lives of premature babies and more sophisticated instruments for earlier identification of developmental delays. Also, there is greater awareness of the irreparable prenatal effects of alcohol and drug abuse by the mother. School districts must provide services to children in the "least restrictive" environment. As school buildings become overcrowded, districts look for a variety of ways to assist in the education of their special-needs constituency. Leasing space or mainstreaming these children into pre-existing early education programs may be a very cost-effective route for schools.

Partnerships with Government Agencies

Whenever a church decides to enter a partnership with a government agency, both parties need to be well aware of the limitations of this partnership. Clear legal understanding and interpretation is essential, especially regarding the "nonestablishment" clause of the first amendment of the Constitution. The government cannot prevent people from practicing their religion. Neither can the government promote the establishment of any one religion. When churches are perceived as serving the general public good, they are usually permitted monies to provide services as part of their ministry. There is a strict separation when churches are seen as educational institutions. Churches must weigh carefully the advantages and disadvantages of receiving government funding as part of implementing their vision of ministry.

Churches may want to help provide for the educational needs of their community but find that a government partnership is too restrictive for their concept of ministry. Other options to address these needs include private schools, home schools, tutoring, a children's library, and lessons or special events in the creative or performing arts.

Guidelines for Partnerships

Whenever the church chooses to serve in partnership with another group, there should be some clearly stated guidelines. This information will enhance the relationship and build the program as part of the entire children's ministry. Five areas have been addressed in the book *Congregations and Child Care* as follows:

* The ministry statement of the program should fit into the larger mission of the church. This should be clearly communicated to the whole church.

* Governance of the program should be clearly established so all concerned understand the extent of their responsibilities and where final authority for decisions lie.

* The leaders of both program and congregation take the responsibility for assuring legal and financial commitments.

* Liaison relationships are established and supported through regular communication and coordination.

* Understanding is established regarding the financial needs and responsibilities of the program and the church.

Tomorrow is known only to the extent that today's mission is clear. The Christian community's mission with children set forth in the previous pages can help create a new generation of adults who will live as "human beings," not "human doers." They will be persons who have discovered reconciliation with God, with themselves, with others, and with creation. They will take seriously the whole person, not simply the spiritual dimension or physical dimension. They will reach out with a new sense of caring for the hurting and hopeless. They will wrestle with concerns and seek justice for all. They will know what to do and what to *stop* doing in order to be!

Epilogue

A Tribute
to the Reverend Watkins

Yes, Reverend Watkins, you did minister in the lives of children. You led your congregation in stating its mission with children. You guided the choice of programs. You helped determine what and how we taught. You spoke strongly for parents and children in meetings when resources, human and financial, were allocated. You encouraged the church to form a partnership with parents.

You invested your life in those who will outlive you!

Listen as the children (including Bill and Jane's four-year-old) sing. They changed words to their favorite song. It's to wish you well as you move to a new place of ministry.

Reverend Watkins, do you know,
That we really love you so?
Little children you have taught
Telling of Jesus' words and thought.
Yes, we do love you,
Yes, we do love you,
Yes, we do love you,
And we'll miss you so.

We're so happy through and through
That we've gotten to know you.
People everywhere you go
Will see the love of God you show.
Yes, we love Jesus,
Yes, we love Jesus,
Yes, we love Jesus,
Because you love Him so.

We will surely miss your smile
That you've brought us for a while,
Thank you for the hours you spent,
And the loving heart you've lent.
Yes, you are special,
Yes, you are special,
Yes, you are special,
Because you loved us so.

Appendix 1:

Designing Nursery Space

The following information can help leaders in evaluating, designing, or remodeling nursery space. Review the information below. Before making any decision, however, ask these questions in priority order: Is it safe? sanitary? secure? sane? and stimulating?

LOCATION
Have area conveniently located to the corporate worship area, but on the walk-out level of the building for immediate evacuation in an emergency.

SIZE
Provide a minimum of thirty-five square feet of usable floor space per child to maintain recommended early-childhood program standards.

COLOR
Use soft earth tones on walls and carpet. The neutrality of walls and floors helps to minimize

distractions and provides a quiet background so colorful toys can be easily seen. Decorations of cool blues and exciting reds can visually divide space for activities such as rest and play.

FLOORING
Wall-to-wall carpeting is a preferred choice for flooring. It provides a warmer surface for the children and helps to absorb sound. Sections of the room can have vinyl flooring to provide a different feel for little feet and knees. It also can be a focal point for the child to learn "This is where I sit to have a cracker and drink."

DOORS
Plan doorways wide enough for cribs to slide through in an emergency. Many nurseries use Dutch doors. Local fire codes should be checked for what is acceptable.

WALLS
Protected pictures and nonbreakable mirrors should be at the child's eye level. Other pictures or mobiles can be at an adult height and introduced to children when carried by a caregiver.

LIGHTING
The crib area should have a separate lighting switch. A dimmer switch adjusts overhead lighting, or small nursery lamps may be used.

VENTILATION
Invest in an exhaust fan or a small rotating fan that can be mounted securely near the ceiling for circulation of air. The quiet hum can produce a soothing sound in the crib area.

SANITATION
Provide easy access to running water and toilets. Tightly covered trash containers are essential.

CRIBS
The distance between crib slats should be less than the width of three adult fingers. Space cribs two feet apart unless they are against a wall. They should never be stacked.

EQUIPMENT
Furnishings and major materials should last at least three years. Keep built-ins to a minimum to allow flexibility. When making purchases, consider the ages and safety needs of the children and adults who will use the room.

STORAGE
In an infant-toddler room, "out-of-reach" is anything over four feet from the floor. Except those cabinets, shelves, and baskets containing toys, all items should be out of reach. Closed cabinets should be child-proofed or locked. Harmful substances, particularly cleaning supplies, should be stored in a separate location.

ROOM ARRANGEMENT
Plan the room arrangement to provide areas for different uses and convenience. Separate sleeping babies from active toddlers. Avoid the tendency to place all the cabinets and containers along the walls. Have safe divisions between those children who are not mobile and those engaged in lots of physical activity. Use large boxes, sturdy barriers, gates, and corrals to provide smaller spaces and interesting nooks for younger children to crawl around, into, and through.

Appendix 2:

Incorporating New Parents

A ministry team can be developed that seeks to meet the needs of this particular group. They may provide pre-parenting classes, which are useful in creating a feeling of belonging and support. Besides disseminating information on safety and health care at home, churches can demonstrate how they provide a safe environment in the church. Expectant parents can spend time in the church nursery to gain awareness of the caregiving techniques. They can also meet with other persons who have young babies or who have had many good experiences with infants.

This team also makes formal announcement and provides recognition of the birth of the baby via the church bulletin or newsletter and places a rosebud on the altar for later presentation to the parents. In addition, this team could enroll the family in the nursery program, so that written materials about family life and child development will be sent periodically and the nursery will be prepared to greet the child and parent when they come to church. This team may also provide social experiences such as a welcoming coffee for the new family, parents' meetings, a baby shower, or some free babysitting coupons that members of the team will gladly redeem. Through all these contacts, the church is showing itself as a "great good place" to be. It is a loving and caring Body of Christ in both word and action.

Additionally, this team helps prepare the family for the child's formal welcome into the community of faith through the service of baptism or dedication. At this time the local church covenants with the parents to assist them in their responsibilities for their child's spiritual welfare. In addition to worship and learning experiences, the church needs to consider informal connections and networking with other churches and organizations. Spiritual development does not take place separately from other areas of development, including the physical, emotional, social, and intellectual.

Bibliography

Accreditation Criteria and Procedures. Washington, D.C.: National Association for the Education of Young Children, 1984.

Barber, Lucie W. *The Religious Education of the Preschool Child.* Birmingham, Ala.: Religious Education Press, 1981.

Benson, Peter L., and Eklin, Carolyn H. *Effective Christian Education: A National Study of Protestant Congregations.* Minneapolis: Search Institute, 1990.

Bower, Bobbie. *Infant-Toddler Ministry.* Chicago: Department of Christian Education and Discipleship, The Evangelical Covenant Church, 1988.

Brown, Lowell E. *Sunday School Standards: A Guide for Achieving Sunday School Success.* Ventura, Calif.:

Bibliography

International Center for Learning, Gospel Light Publications, 1986.

Drucker, Peter. *Managing a Non-profit Organization.* New York: Harper Collins, 1990.

Evaluating Curriculum Materials. Chicago: Department of Christian Education and Discipleship, The Evangelical Covenant Church, 1991.

In the Eye of the Storm: Liability Insurance and Child Care—Policy Report #2. New York: Child Advocacy Office, National Council of the Churches of Christ in the United States of America.

Oldenburg, Ray. *The Great Good Place.* New York: Paragon House, 1989.

Schaller, Lyle. *It's a Different World.* Nashville: Abingdon Press, 1987.

Seymour, Jack. "A Reforming Movement: The Story of Protestant Sunday School," *Renewing Sunday School and CCD.* D. Campbell Wyckoff, ed. Birmingham, Ala.: Religious Education Press, 1986.

Silver, Rosalind, ed. *Media and Values.* Number 52-53. Fall 1990/Winter 1991.

Steele, Dorothy M. *Congregations and Child Care.* New York: The National Council of Churches Child Advocacy Office, 1990.